BEING
Pastor
IN AN
ANXIOUS
SOCIETY

Primix Publishing
11620 Wilshire Blvd
Suite 900, West Wilshire Center, Los Angeles, CA, 90025
www.primixpublishing.com
Phone: 1-800-538-5788

Published by Primix Publishing: 03/25/2024

ISBN: 979-8-89194-106-9(sc)
ISBN: 979-8-89194-107-6(e)

Library of Congress Control Number: 2024901986

PRIMIX
PUBLISHING
THE WRITE CHOICE

STEPHEN McCUTCHAN

BEING *Pastor* IN AN ANXIOUS SOCIETY

LIVING IN AN AGE OF DISTRUST

We are living in a society where no one trusts anyone? The purpose of institutions is to help us organize and bring coherence to our lives. We depend on laws to protect us and make society fair. We have organizations that provide a pattern that we can count on. Let me list several of the major institutions that serve to organize and bind our society together and see if you cannot immediately suggest at least one major incident in recent times that has shattered people's ability to place trust in that institution.

TAKE THE TEST

- Financial and investment institutions.
- Government--locally and nationally.
- Medical--doctors, hospitals, research.
- Educational institutions--elementary, high school, college, graduate.
- Justice--police, courts, lawyers, etc.
- Insurance--both private and corporate.
- Corporations--large and small.
- Religion--congregations, denominations, interfaith.
- Charities--both in collection and
- Social Service agencies--working with all age groups.
- Social media-- TV and radio networks, internet groups, newspapers.
- Contractors--Builders, repair groups, architects, engineers.

THE CHALLENGE

A central question for our society is who do you trust? I've named a dozen institutions, but you could add to the list. Every day we hear about someone being hacked or scammed. How do you live in a healthy manner in a society in which scandals and scams have shattered people's ability to trust? For those who either work in or participate in a religious institution, how do you help people learn to navigate through this maze of distrust and not become isolated and alienated? That is a central challenge for Christians whose faith insists on our being part of a community of truth and reconciliation.

What happens when you can no longer trust a institution to fulfill its intended purpose? Is it any wonder that our society is filled with cynicism?People often feel like helpless victims.Increasingly we either read about or witness people erupting in bizarre behavior. They have lost the ability to trust anyone except a few individuals near to them.

I am fully aware that churches are among the institutions that have been plagued with scandals by both their members and their spiritual leaders. While I don't agree with those who want to claim to be spiritual but not religious, I certainly understand their response.

However, building Paul's quotation from God in 1 Corinthians 12:9 "My grace is sufficient for you, for my power is made perfect in weakness," I believe that we can nurture healthy spiritual leadership that can enable healthy congregations to provide renewed hope and courage in our society.

WE ARE NOT ALONE

Our faith begins with an act of trust. Abram trusted God and began the journey that changed the world. The biblical journey continues to tell the story of how people of faith demonstrate trust first in God, next in the community of the faithful, and finally in responding to the society in which they live. Jesus trusted God even as he faced the cross.

While we need to make our political decisions and participate in many of the institutions that glue our society together, most of us are not in a position to significantly alter people's trust in those institutions. What we can do is seek to affect people's experience of trust in our congregations and through that, change their core attitude as they engage with the larger society. Imagine the impact if the people of our churches and congregations began to develop a central core of trust in themselves and their God that grounded them as they live in this society. Try to think of some beginning steps you could take that might affect your neighbor's trust level in the religious community in which you participate.

TRUST AND OBEY: MOST CHRISTIANS PREFER ANOTHER WAY.

Let us begin by being honest about our history. Despite Jesus' commandment that we love one another so that the world will believe that God had sent Jesus, Christians historically have chosen another way. Here is a game I developed to engage a congregation in discussing the conflicts that divide us.

DISCUSSING CONFLICT IN THE FAITH

Engage your membership in an exchange around the topic of conflicts in the church. Whether by email or in an assembly, ask them to consider this question::

When you hear about or even experience conflict in either the local or national church, how does it make you feel? Do you want to say, "If the church was truly Christian, there would not be any conflict."?

After they have responded, share the following. Would it surprise you to know that conflict in the church began with the disciples? It is recorded among Jesus' first disciples. "An argument arose among them as to which one of them was the greatest." (Luke 9:46) Lest you think that was just an early weakness that was overcome, later Luke records right after Jesus had instituted the Lord's Supper "A dispute also arose among them as to which one of them was to be regarded as the greatest." (Luke 22:24) The struggle continues, as seen in the writings of Paul. "Now I appeal to you, brothers and sisters, by the name of our Lord Jesus Christ, that all of you be in agreement and that there be no divisions among you, but that you be united in the same mind and the same purpose." (1 Corinthians 1:10)

WHAT CAUSED THE CHURCH TO SPLIT?

I want to invite you to play a game. The first stage of the game goes like this. I will identify eight historical arguments given for church division and identify three major splits in the historical church. You are asked to see if you can identify which causes are associated with which major church separations.

THE THREE MAJOR HISTORIC DIVISIONS IN THE CHRISTIAN CHURCH ARE:

A: The Great Schism of 1054 that split the Eastern Orthodoxy and the Western Roman Catholic Church,

B: The Protestant Reformation,

C: The division between the Anglican Church and the Methodist Church.

Match up the issues that led to at least one of these divisions:

- Who is responsible for the proper ordination of candidates for the ministry?
- Should the leaders of the church speak the same language?
- Should the Eucharist bread be leavened or unleavened?
- To what degree does your behavior determine your salvation?
- should we emphasize Jesus Christ's humanity or his divinity?
- Should assistance to the poor be a major or minor focus?
- What style of worship is appropriate for the church?
- Should members of the church be asked to pledge loyalty to a power beyond their nation's government?

If you discuss this with others, you will discover that most believers can't begin to explain the issues that separate different denominations, but they still experience

the shame of the split Body of Christ.

HOW TO TRUST WHEN YOU CAN'T VERIFY

Ronald Reagan famously coined the phrase that you should trust and verify. Whether he was right in the world of international relations, it is a far different reality when it comes to the faith journey. The core of our faith journey is based on our relationship with God and neighbor.

Begin with the neighbor. When you think about it, few things can destroy our relationship with another human being more than the constant attempt to verify our relationship. Whether it is a spouse or a friend, consider the impact of continually checking up on them. "Where are you going, dear? Who are you talking to on the phone? How much did you spend on that purchase?"

When it comes to God, trying to verify your relationship with God quickly becomes a form of idolatry. God becomes an object which we observe and a force we seek to control.

The bonds of true relationships are based on trust. If we need to test the relationship, we are insisting the party prove their value to us. This is the essence of the second temptation Jesus faced. Can God or neighbor prove their loyalty to us. We set the criteria.

LETTING GOD BE GOD

When you think about the biblical characters of our faith, each one of them had to learn that God was free of human attempts to control. From Abraham and Sarah to Jesus as he walked towards the cross, the visible markers that humans might use to verify God's faithfulness were not available. The elderly Abram and Sarai were childless and had to begin their journey trusting God. Death seemed the final marker of defeat for Jesus, and the cross appeared to be a sign of failure. God refuses to fit into our small boxes of what is possible. To trust God is to step out into the future and take the risk that God will be there, even in ways that seem impossible from the human perspective.

DO YOU SUPPOSE GOD HAS A BETTER WAY FOR PEOPLE OF FAITH TO RESPOND TO CONFLICT AMONG THEM?

As the Bible reports, we don't have to be perfect to allow God to work through us and our faith community. We just need to be open to God's spirit in a healthy manner.

Let us look at both unhealthy and healthy ways to respond to the anxiety of our society.

UNHEALTHY SYMPTOMS IN ANXIOUS CHURCH

Let us identify what <u>behavior</u> looks like in an <u>unhealthy church</u>. This is not a judgment but a recognition that all churches have both healthy and unhealthy behaviors. Many of these <u>unhealthy behaviors</u> are a reflection of people's response to their anxiety and distrust in their world which is carried over to their participation in the church.

First, make at least <u>three statements</u> that describe symptoms of anxiety in our larger society. Think of the <u>behavior and fears</u> that reflect feelings of anxiety.How do people speak or act because they are feeling anxious?

Second, if people brought their feelings of anxiety into a church community, how might the three behaviors described reflect an attempt to address those feelings of anxiety? At this point, think of <u>any church</u>. Make at least <u>four statements</u> in response. If people feel anxious,they might act in this way.

Now, rate <u>your church</u> in terms of the behavior of individuals or groups in their effort to address the anxiety of their community. Taking each of the three descriptions of behavior, use #1 to suggest that never happens and #10 to indicate that this always reflects behavior in our church. The behavior may be that of an individual, a small interest group, the governing body, or the whole church.

IMAGE OF AN UNHEALTHY CHURCH

LET'S TALK ABOUT SIGNS OF UNHEALTHINESS IN OUR CHURCH

When people feel anxious, it makes them feel vulnerable. In order to numb the fears generated by a sense of vulnerability, unhealthy churches tend to:

1. **Demand certainty** in the face of uncertainty. We don't want ambiguous answers to our questions but clear proclamation of definite answers. Give me the three ways to heaven, the four habits that will provide a perfect marriage, or the seven steps to prosperity.

2. We **want perfection** in the face of our anxious world. Churches should be perfect, clergy should be perfect, denominations should be perfect. If something goes wrong, it is clearly because someone is incompetent. Get rid of them, and everything will be all right again.

3. We pretend that what we do as a church is our own business and **doesn't impact others**. We don't determine doctrine according to its impact on those it excludes. We don't design our buildings according to how it affects the neighborhood. We don't consider the impact of our budget decisions as a testimony to the larger world.

Being anxious is not wrong. There are plenty of reasons why people might have their anxiety level raised. However, there are healthy and unhealthy ways to behave in light of that anxiety.

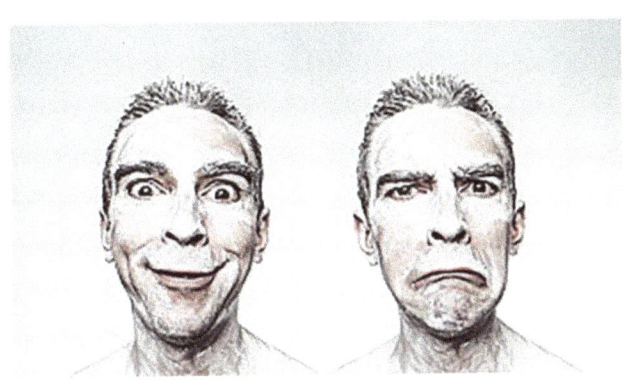

IMAGES OF HEALTHY CHURCH IN ANXIOUS TIMES

Healthy churches believe that they are not worthy by what they do but **by God's grace they are made worthy,**
CONSIDER THESE FIVE CHARACTERISTICS:

1. Healthy churches have the **courage to be imperfect**. They tell an honest story of a people who are willing to *live the question* without having all the answers. Like Abraham and Sarah, they are on a journey without knowing the final destination but trusting in the God who leads them.

2. They are **not defensive about their faults** but are willing to explore them honestly so that they might grow from them towards maturity in Christ. They know the biblical story of how God chooses to work through imperfect people--Abraham, David, the Disciples, Saul, and the list continues throughout all of church history.

3. Their practices emphasize a **blending of gratitude and joy**. They are grateful they have been invited on the journey. Doubt and questions are simply the boundaries on the edge of growth.

4. They trust that being vulnerable to others and God is the **birthplace of creativity, compassion, joy, belonging, and love**. Therefore, healthy churches are not afraid to fail. They dare to let God use their offerings for great things for the world God loves.

5. They believe in and **practice connectivity.** Faith well lived is lived in community among imperfect people who choose to exercise their hope in community. After all the doctrinal debates, they know that it boils down to relationships as Jesus declared in the Great Commandment.

With each of the five characteristics of a healthy church listed, try to give three examples of how a church might reflect that behavior. Begin with an abstract church. Later you can apply it to your particular church. For example, what might a person or church do to reflect the courage to be imperfect? Can you think of other biblical examples of people having the courage to be imperfect?

As you discuss the image of a healthy church, consider the relationship of churches to each other. We are called to be the **One Body of Christ**. What are some specific ways that churches might relate to each other, in small groups and as a whole body that would offer a healthy witness?

Identify some simple steps that the churches in your community might take that would strengthen their capacity to be a healthy witness to the world around them.

How might you relate to a church significantly larger or smaller?
What about a church that probably is more liberal or conservative?
Consider a church in a distinctly different denomination.
Identify a church whose membership reflects a different ethnic or economic status.

Choose simple steps that you could act on this year.

LET US LOOK AT THE SPIRITUAL LEADERSHIP
THAT GOD INVITES US TO OFFER.

HOW TO PASTOR IN AN ANXIOUS CONGREGATION

(I am drawing upon Brene' Brown's work on vulnerability and applying it to the work of ministry.)

Anxiety is a response to what William Butler Yeats spoke of in his poem *The Second Coming:* "Things fall apart, the center does not hold." When we feel the ground shift beneath our feet, whether personally or globally, it is as if we have lost control. Our sense of security dims, and we begin to feel helpless to affect the outcome. We have been examining the evidence of distrust in our society that has left us with a pervasive experience of anxiety.

THREE BASIC RESPONSES TO ANXIETY

Brown suggests that there are three basic responses that communities make in response to feeling anxious and vulnerable.

1. **They want to make uncertainty into certainties .**

They are not interested in questioning, exploring, or theorizing about problems. They want answers-Clear, direct, unambiguous answers. The popularity of fundamentalism and the rise of cults build on that need for certainty in an age of uncertainty. Someone must know the inside secret to how we can solve our problems.

2. **They measure things, people, institutions, and communities by the criteria of perfection. I repeat them here for emphasis.**

Things should be perfect. If they are not perfect, someone else is being evil. There are no excuses. Only perfection is acceptable. We want our children to be perfect, our spouses to be perfect, our doctors, business people, and politicians to be perfect, and mistakes are not acceptable.

Grace is a nice concept, but we expect our pastors to be perfect pastors and our churches to be successful in all their programs.

3. They **refuse to accept responsibility for the consequences of their decisions on other people's lives.**

In times of anxiety, most people are less interested in how the church can make a decision or take action that will help the vulnerable beyond their church community than they are in how the church can benefit the membership.

The more anxious they are, the less interested members are in hearing that love of neighbor includes the stranger and the vulnerable in society.

HEALTHY CLERGY MAKE HEALTHY CONGREGATIONS

CLERGY DON'T HAVE IT ALL TOGETHER

Clergy, like all humans, come to their work with all the wounds, hungers, insecurities, and troubles of their past. As the Bible makes clear, being called by God does not perfect the person. As our seminaries demonstrate, you don't perfect a person through education. We are the imperfect servants of God through whom God chooses to work to effect the divine purpose.

So, when I say *Healthy Clergy Make Healthy Congregations*, I recognize that we are at best speaking of *Wounded Healers*. However, a vital issue for clergy is whether they can respond to the unhealthy dynamics they encounter in a congregation and ministry in a healthy manner.

EMBRACING THE CHRIST WITHIN US

IMPERFECT CLERGY/HEALTHY RESPONSES

Consider some of the healthy responses that clergy can make in a congregation.

HOW DO WE DO THAT?

HOW TO PASTOR TO AN ANXIOUS COMMUNITY

Whether it is Moses as he faced the Red Sea, the Disciples following the crucifixion, or the church in our time, all are called to proclaim boldly a message of hope in a sea of uncertainty. There are no easy answers, and we are to be faithful in the face of an impossible task. Yet we as clergy bring our own anxieties and fears of vulnerability as we engage in ministry.

As shown in the stories of the faith community in the Scriptures, the call was never meant to be an easy task. We are to dare greatly, hold firmly during the storm, and trust that God really does know what God is doing.

A challenge for any pastor in this anxious age is not to absorb the anxiety of the congregation. Anxiety can easily become contagious, and what an anxious church does not need is an anxious pastor. Anxious pastors become their own worst judge. They keep searching for the latest sure-fire plan to grow a congregation, have a successful building campaign, redesign the worship service that will draw the crowds, etc. When the ideas don't work, they judge themselves. That can easily lead to depression or health problems.

3 KEYS TO AVOIDING BEING AN ANXIOUS PASTOR

1. NOT BEING DRAWN INTO ANXIETY

A NEW FORM OF SABBATH

According to Genesis, after six days of labor at creating the world, God took a sabbath to step back and view what he had done and where God was going from there. In practical terms, the Sabbath provides an opportunity to breathe, evaluate, and envision.

This is the Sabbath that a pastor should engage in on a regular basis. At least every two weeks, a pastor should mark off a couple of hours for Sabbath time. Go to a park, a coffee shop, a library, or even a parlor in a friend's church.

First take some time in prayer breathing in the Spirit of God and reminding yourself that God has called you.

Second, allow the last several months to float through your mind like a movie. Make a note of both the satisfying and the stressing moments in your life.

Then, ask yourself where God was present as a part of both the positive and negative moments that you are viewing.

Third, building on your belief that God is calling you to ministry, begin asking yourself what possibilities might lie ahead in the next several months. How might God be leading you to respond to the congregation in a way that might ease their anxiety?

Don't try to be too specific in those thoughts. Just let them flow through your mind.

Close with some time in prayer where you offer up your thoughts to God and ask that God might be with you as you continue in your ministry. Mark in your calendar the next time you are going to take a Sabbath breather. Don't neglect this step because it can easily slip away if you are not intentional about taking a regular Sabbath break.

2. OVERCOMING CYNICISM IN THE CHURCH

A remarkable feature in the biblical story, including the disciples and stories of the early church, is the refusal to whitewash the lives of our spiritual leaders. Unlike our society that tends to deny and hide their failures, the Bible emphasizes the power of confession and forgiveness. Peter's denial and Saul/Paul's violent attack on the church were transformed by God into a saving reality.

BEGIN WITH CONFESSION

Trusting God begins with confessing our inability to save ourselves both as individuals and as a community. It would be a healthy exercise for a church community, both as a denomination and as congregations, to identify some of their past failures and explore together how God has continued to bear witness to a saving truth through the church.

Consider urging your congregation to reflect on how that same faithfulness of God has plays out in the history of both their church and the denominations in our society.

3. A VISION FOR A CONGREGATION

Consider some central theological concepts that a pastor might draw upon for the congregation and for self. These can be emphasized in sermons, conversation, and proposed actions by the congregation. You are seeking to reflect how people of faith live in an anxious society.

- An emphasis on the sovereignty of God. In an uncertain world, people need to be reminded that we believe that God is Lord of history. It is God, not the politicians, personal wealth, or bright ideas that we look to for the future. If our prayer is accurate, "Thy will be done on EARTH as it is in heaven," then we are looking for that hope in our earthly life. Human institutions do let us down, but God can be trusted.
- Humans, even the best of humans, are imperfect. That goes for our institutions as well. We don't need to look for the perfect politician, preacher, or church to save us. We need to look for ways that imperfect people can build community and support each other in building a better life.
- Like Abraham and Sarah, when they began this venture of faith, we are on a journey without a clear set of answers but with a God who we can trust. Naturally, we will make mistakes and even suffer a little. But on the way, we can experience joy, creativity, and belonging. We are not alone, and if we are compassionate to each other, we will be led to a better place.

HOW CAN GOD USE OUR CHURCH COMMUNITY?

WHAT WOULD IT LOOK LIKE?

THREE KEY COMMANDMENTS AS AN ANTITOXIN TO ANXIETY FOR OUR PEOPLE

NO OTHER GODS

It is the first commandment, but it is interesting how quickly people pass it by. It is so easy to make other gods, golden calves, when we are anxious because our leaders have let us down. Wasn't that what the people did when Moses was gone too long, and the people thought they were abandoned. Whether it is a cult, a politician, a get rich quick scheme, or some famous person, we keep looking for someone to save us.

REMEMBER THE SABBATH DAY

Far too often, we think of the Sabbath commandment as having to do with going to church or blue laws that have been mostly abolished in our society. Businesses brag that they are a 24/7 business, as if that has merit.

The Sabbath commandment is a command to stop depending on other gods for our happiness. Once a week, we are to stop trying to produce, achieve, or build ourselves up. We are to take time out to relate to God and neighbor. We re to pause and reflect on the meaning of life. We are to set aside anxiety for a day, trust God, and enjoy life.

WE ARE NOT ALONE, AND WE HAVE REASON TO HOPE

HONOR YOUR FATHER AND YOUR MOTHER

Our parents and our ancestors were not perfect. In fact, when you reflect on some of the history that brought us to this point, there are many factors for which we should be ashamed. However, from a faith perspective, it is significant to recall that God worked through these imperfect people to achieve the Divine purpose. Whether we begin with Adam and Eve or with Abraham and Sarah, as we follow the faith story, we recognize that God tends to choose to work with imperfect people. They were not people who had all the answers, were always ethically perfect, or were clear about how to relate to their neighbors. When we honor them, we recognize that imperfect people accomplish incredible things.

If we trust in one God to act as faithfully as God has done in the past, regularly interrupt our anxious pursuit of survival long enough to reflect on and reconnect with God and with the others on the journey with us, and acknowledge the shame but recognize the redemptive faith of our ancestors, then there is reason not to be anxious.

A COMMUNITY OF HEALTHY TRUST

BIBLICAL JOURNEY OF TRUST

A major theme running throughout the biblical story is the theme of trust. Trust involves risk. Consider the beginning of our faith story with the call of Abram and Sarai. When they were called to leave behind all that gave them security and move out on the adventure that resulted in our community of faith, they had to trust the one who had called them. We can look back and see the results of their decision, but it began with a risk and no guarantees.

THE RISK FACTOR

You will find the same combination of decision making and taking risks as part of the journey of other biblical characters.

If you are going to build a community of trust in your congregation, both you and your people need to understand that a faith journey involves both decisions and risk.

A **first step** might be to engage your people through sermons, prayer, and educational events in exploring risk factors that were part of those biblical stories that are the foundation of our community of faith.

What were the decisions made and the risk factors involved in the biblical stories about Abraham, Isaac, and Jacob? Then follow the same questions through the decisions made by other significant biblical figures. Make sure that you carry that process through the lives of those in the New Testament. You might even want to reflect on a similar process as reflected in church history.

ANXIOUS SOCIETY

We live in an anxious society. I identified for you the way that institutional failures in the last fifty years have shattered people's confidence. Living in such an anxious society, people search for certainty. Being isolated from community institutions that they can trust, they are not prepared to take risks that depend upon making sacrifices for the greater good of society. The faith challenge for a community is to begin to take even small steps that risk trusting in God and searching for a healthier response to their neighbors.

As A Beginning

Consider engaging your people, perhaps through a combination of gatherings and Internet conversations, to consider how you might take some risks in faith. As they make their suggestions, encourage them to relate the risks they suggest to parallel risks taken in the biblical story. The advantage of this is that it keeps the people grounded in the faith story as you journey together.

Ask people to suggest possible faith steps, and then through a series of interactions, keeping the combined list for future reference, select a couple of risks the community might take together.

Keep reminding your people that the purpose of such decision making and risk taking is to deepen the spiritual lives of those who are living the faith. We live in a risk-averse society, and fear and negativity often reflect that anxiety. It is in flexing our spiritual muscles that we strengthen ourselves for the journey.

HONORING THE PAST COUNTERS ANXIETY

THE FIFTH COMMANDMENT EXPANDED

We need to reinterpret the fifth commandment. "Honor your father and your mother, so that your days may be long in the land that the Lord your God is giving you" Exodus 20:12. If you read that commandment to your congregation, how many of them would assume that means they should be kind to their biological parents? Of course, out of painful experiences, there will be some who find that commandment very difficult to obey, but probably the majority would assume this is one of the easier commandments to complete.

Do you recall the incident where Jesus was responding to his mother and brothers coming to speak to him, and Jesus replied, "'Who is my mother, and who are my brothers?' And pointing to his disciples, he said, 'Here are my mother and my brothers! For whoever does the will of my Father in heaven is my brother and sister and mother.'" How does that expand your understanding of the commandment? Now honoring your mother and father extends to all those in the congregation present, past, and future.

SPEAKING OF SHAME

While that commandment may be difficult for some people because of painful experiences in their family, the same is true for many in the church. To effectively respond to this commandment, we need to understand the importance of talking about shame. Shame, as Brene' Brown speaks of it, is a fear of not being worthy. Remember, this is different than guilt. Guilt is based on an action--I did something wrong. Shame is a feeling that I am not worthy.

The Biblical story of the community of faith speaks openly about unworthy people being made worthy by God to effect good purpose. Most of the leading figures in the story of faith are deeply flawed but are celebrated because of what God has done through them.

HONORING SHAMEFUL PARENTS

If a congregation is able to speak honestly about their history, they will discover how some very human and flawed people have been used by God to accomplish some amazing things in founding and nurturing their church. Too often, we try to cover up the shameful parts and only talk about the respectable parts. If a pastor can integrate this rocky past into the liturgy of the story of the church's faith journey, s/he is genuinely honoring the parents of the congregation. The pastor is also helping to establish a sense of courage and God-given worth to the present congregation. Suddenly we don't need to arrive at perfection with all the answers to our doubts before we can be the TRUE CHURCH. As God worked through our ancestors, so God can work through us. We are worthy servants, and we don't need to be anxious about our weaknesses. God's power is made perfect through our weakness, (2 Cor 12:9.

PARENTAL COMFORT IN ANXIETY

When we honor our ancestors in our congregation, we are set free of the tyranny of perfection and liberated to dare greatly. We need not be anxious about the future. As a congregation, we should heed Jesus' words, "So do not worry about tomorrow, for tomorrow will bring worries of its own. Today's trouble is enough for today." (Mat 6:34)

CONGREGATIONAL GAME TO BUILD TRUST

Invite the congregation to enjoy a game that builds fun, fellowship, and reflection.

MAJORITY RULES

This is a community-building game adapted to a church community. The set up for the game is this: Place participants in groups of four—perhaps around card tables. Assign each group a number for their group.

Explain that they will be asked a series of questions and that there is not a right answer. The best answer is the answer of the majority of the groups. All of the groups will be asked the same question with four possible answers. Each group will discuss the question and determine the best answer for their group. That answer will be placed on their ballot with the group number identified and sent to the chief judge who will count the votes and determine which answer has the majority of votes.

The groups who answered with the majority will score a point for their group. The process will continue until all of the questions have been voted upon. The winning groups will be identified, and the rest of the groups will rise, bow to the winners, and say, "We hail you o wise ones of our church and salute you for your wisdom."

The judge will share a compilation of the decisions and invite the whole group's response to the picture of the church that has been painted.

ENJOY THE PROCESS

The following questions are suggested for the decision of the majority.

1. <u>To nurture a warm, welcoming church, each member should:</u>

   a. Speak to at least seven people before they leave church.
   b. Take notice of and speak to people they cant call by name.
   c. Always sit in the same place so peopple around them are familiar.
   d. Pray by name for members who seem lonely.

2. <u>To lessen conflict and create harmony, pastors should:</u>
   a. Avoid preaching on Scriptures that might be controversial.
   b. Only preach on subjects about which everyone agrees.

   c. Acknowledge potential disagreements about points made and encourage further conversation.
   d. Allow people to vote on which parts of the Gospel they like and preach accordingly.

3. <u>To build transparency with respect to church finances, the leadership should:</u>
   a. Always report on and invite feedback on major expenditures.
   b. List by name and amount all pledges to the church.
   c. Identify the faith principles you want to proclaim by your budget.
   d. Encourage open conversation about church expenditures as a faith issue.

4. <u>Identify the biggest contributor to distrust among</u> <u>church members.</u>
   a. Inadequate communication.
   b. Feeling that only a few people make all the decisions.
   c. Failure to understand how decisions are made in the church.
   d. Failure to hold a shared vision about the nature and mission of the church.

5. <u>Characteristics of a successful preacher</u>

   a. Ability to popular sermons that inspire but don't offend.
   b. Preaches sermons clearly grounded in the Bible.
   c. Preaches with integrity even when it offends but is open to feedback.
   d. Preaches sermons that address personal issues but avoids commenting on social issues.

6. <u>Cynicism and distrust are reduced in a congregation</u> <u>when:</u>
   a. Diverse opinions are heard and respected.
   b. Controversial issues are not discussed.
   c. People accept that none of their opinions are perfect in God's eyes and continually seek to grow in understanding.
   d. People are committed to a shared vision about the church's mission.

7. The major reason churches split is:

    a. Refuse to accept that we are all sinners and need to continually forgive each other.
    b. Choose to emphasize right beliefs over loving behavior.
    c. Refuse to accept Jesus command that we be one has priority.
    d. Allow personal beliefs to take precedence over being faithful to the church.

8. Loving your enemy is most difficult when:

    a. Your enemy is from a different culture.
    b. Your enemy belongs to your church but has different beliefs.
    c. Your enemy trats you with contempt.
    d. Your enemy affirms a different faith.

9. You know you can trust your pastor if:
    a. S/he totally agrees with your opinions.
    b. S/he is interprets Scripture and faith with total integrity.
    c. S/he prays daily to be faithful and obedient to God.
    d. S/he is unafraid to preach with integrity, but listens sensitively to those who disagree.

ADDRESSING A CONGREGATION'S ANXIETY

WORDS CREATE WORLDS

In Walter Brueggemann's *Israel's Praise,* he develops the idea that *words create worlds.* It is not the objective experiences we have but the way we interpret those experiences that constitute the world in which we live. If I am a dietician, I see food as relating to the world of health. If I am a chef who continually is reading about new recipes, then I see food in terms of taste. If I manage a restaurant, then I see food in terms of cost. In lay terms, the words that fill our lives become the spectacles through which we see and interpret the world of experiences around us.

LITURGY CREATES WORLDS

Every week people step out of their various worlds of finance, Internet, business, law, government, medicine, etc. and gather together to participate in saying a different set of words. In effect, through liturgy, we offer a different perspective, a different world, through which to interpret our experiences. It often challenges the other worlds that people inhabit. How do you explain a world in which God exists, grace is experienced, forgiveness is a viable option, and generosity is encouraged? Liturgy is not just a set of words to mumble through before we get to the sermon. Liturgy offers us an alternative world through which we interpret our experiences.

LITURGY AND ANXIETY

Anxious people come into our churches. They are prepared to act in the church out of their world of anxiety. You have the opportunity to provide them words in liturgy that counter the toxic effect of anxiety in their lives.

Stop for a moment and consider at least three to five basic ideas of faith that, if truly believed, would act as a counter to the anxiety they are feeling. For example, with many of our institutions failing to live up to their promise, it is easy to join the Tea Party and trust no one and no institution—particularly not the government. If you are convinced that God is sovereign and continually works through imperfect people to accomplish good purposes, as the Bible suggests, how would that alter how you interpreted what is happening in the world? If you *sang Christ Is Made the Sure Foundation,* how would that affect your feelings of despair? How does praying "Forgive us our debts as we forgive our debtors" affect your inclinations as you respond to some of the conflicts you experience in your life?

Our anxiety and sense of vulnerability quickly leads to us wanting to find fault with others, demand perfection around us, and become less sensitive to our neighbors. Consider litanies that emphasize God's sovereignty, grace, hope in the face of the impossible, and the power of love to transform. Consider the power of prayers of thanksgiving to alter our fears of scarcity and experience the joy of having been blessed.

A PASTOR'S STRATEGY

As a pastor, you have the power to shape liturgies that emphasize the core doctrines of our faith that counteract the toxic effect of our anxieties. Begin with yourself. What are the forces and events that are causing you to feel anxious? Then think of the fundamental doctrines of faith that counter that vulnerability. Finally, begin to integrate those faith ideas into the various parts of the liturgy. Create liturgies using faith words through which your members can interpret their experiences in the world. It will be strengthened if you develop in sermons declaring how those ideas of faith can become a shield against the principalities and powers that threaten us.

IT HELPS TO LAUGH

On my website, www.smccutchan.com, you will find *God Laughs-Why Don't You?: Making Use of Humor in the Practice of Ministry.* bit.ly/Godlaughs In many ways it may be the most unusual book that I have written in my effort to provide helpful resources for the pastor engaged in ministry.

This book is dedicated to the clergy of the world who commit themselves to being God's spokesperson to humanity and interceding with God on behalf of humanity. It is written with the full awareness that the more sensitive clergy are to both God and humanity, the more demanding their own lives become. It is offered with the hope that for some exercising humor in their lives can be experienced as God's healing gift.

INTERRUPTING THE STRESS OF MINISTRY

Being an ordained minister in our culture is a stressful challenge. We can take ourselves far too seriously and forget that we are humans called by God to serve a higher purpose, and as God reminded Paul, "My grace is sufficient for you, for my power is made perfect in weakness" (2 Cor 12:9). Spiritually, laughter at self can help remind us that we are not God, and salvation depends not on our perfection but on God's grace.

Sometimes it helps to remind ourselves of the ridiculous paradox in which we find ourselves as ordained clergy.

It's tough being a pastor these days.

Who is your boss?

God calls you.

A denomination ordains you.

A congregation hires you.

Who is Your boss?

HEALTHY SOULS CAN LAUGH

Grace is frustrating.
No matter how gifted you are,
You can't win God's popularity contest.

I'm in support of God's grace in my life.
I even think it is a nice boost to some people who are down.
I just wish God would check with me first to see who is worthy.

Who is your boss?

Jesus says, "You cannot serve God and wealth."

The **congregation** says, "Can't you attract some rich bankers and lawyers to help the budget."

God says, "I sent my son to proclaim Good News to the poor and lift up the brokenhearted."

The **congregation** says, "Too many bums are coming to this church to get help, and it's ruining our reputation."

Paul says, "For freedom, Christ has set us free. . .. The whole law is summed up in a single commandment, 'You shall love your neighbor as yourself.'"

The **denomination** says, "These are the rules. Obey them or move."

PARTNERS WITH GOD

God said, "I'll create humans with free will."

Satan sneered, "I'll defeat you with sin (ego, pride)

God said, "I'll send my son, who will live a perfect life of faith."

Death snickered, "I'll crucify him."

God said, "I'll save the world with churches led by very human pastors."

Hope laughed, "This I got to see. Can I help?"

God said, "Only if you have a sense of humor."

**Maybe a laugh a day can keep the
demons away.**

The book concludes with a section <u>A Pastor's Survival Notebook</u> which offers practical advice on how to utilize humor in your life and ministry.

YOU ARE PART OF AN AWE-FILLED AND NOBLE CALLING

It is not easy to be a pastor in an anxious society but look at God's call from God's perspective. Step aside from your personal situation and try to write several statements about what it means to be called by God. I'll provide several that I can think of, and then you try to write out several of your own.

TO BE CALLED BY GOD MEANS:

- To feel a genuine connection between your life and God's purpose.
- To sense that your work, even that which seems insignificant, is part of something larger than yourself.
- To believe God can work through you to bring God back into the lives of others.
- To help others find meaning in their personal lives.
- To be an advocate for God's justice, love, and mercy.

LIVING IN THE QUESTION

Basil Pennington, in his book, *Living in the Question,* suggests that the conditions and challenges that shake us out of our comfort zone can be rich opportunities for us to listen more deeply to God. The very questions that occur to you about God's call may be an opportunity to probe more deeply your understanding of what God is saying to you. If you reflect on the disciples, it is clear that God has a penchant for working with very ordinary people to accomplish Godly intentions. Accept as an assumption that God knows who you are, what your strengths and weaknesses are, and the context in which you are exercising your ministry. Take either a pen and paper or your computer and write for fifteen minutes a dialogue between you and God in which God explains to you what the possibilities are in your ministry. You may want to begin your part of the conversation by resisting God's reasons--after all, that is what Moses did. Then watch the exchange unfold.

Now it's your turn. Stretch yourself to write at least five more. Look at our combined list and note how it feels to be part of being called by God.

There is more to examining God's call in your life, but this is a good beginning.

THANK YOU FOR RESPONDING TO GOD'S CALL IN YOUR LIFE.

MAY YOU BE BLESSED

Because you love the church,
imagine if you could help yourself and other clergy
with these resources: All available at
www.smccutchan.com

A Company of Pastors--overcoming isolation and loneliness
An Interim Pastor's Gift--a healthy beginning for new clergy
God Laughs, Why Don't You--humor as antidote to stress
Clergy Physical Health--keeping the body healthy
Clergy Emotional Health--staying emotionally centered
Clergy Family Health--Positive family response to ministry
Clergy Financial Health--Positive response to finances
Clergy Spiritual Health--Spiritual growth in all circumstances
Clergy Vocational Health--Staying in touch with your call

Healthy
Clergy
Make
Healthy
Congregations

www.ingramcontent.com/pod-product-compliance
Lightning Source LLC
Chambersburg PA
CBHW041525120626
46551CB00018B/2578